How to...
BUILD
A ROCKET

By HAZEL RICHARDSON

Illustrated by
Scoular Anderson

OXFORD
UNIVERSITY PRESS

For my father, the original mad inventor

OXFORD
UNIVERSITY PRESS

Great Clarendon Street, Oxford OX2 6DP

Oxford University Press is a department of the University of Oxford.
It furthers the University's objective of excellence in research, scholarship,
and education by publishing worldwide in

Oxford New York

Athens Auckland Bangkok Bogotá Buenos Aires Calcutta
Cape Town Chennai Dar es Salaam Delhi Florence Hong Kong Istanbul
Karachi Kuala Lumpur Madrid Melbourne Mexico City Mumbai
Nairobi Paris São Paulo Singapore Taipei Tokyo Toronto Warsaw

with associated companies in Berlin Ibadan

Oxford is a registered trade mark of Oxford University Press
in the UK and in certain other countries

Text copyright © Hazel Richardson 1999

The moral rights of the author and the artist have been asserted

First published 1999

British Library Cataloguing in Publication Data available

ISBN 0-19-910591-X

1 3 5 7 9 10 8 6 4 2

Cover illustration: Andy Cooke

Printed and bound in Great Britain
by Cox & Wyman Ltd, Reading, Berkshire

Contents

Introduction

Why build a rocket?   6

Chapter One

What is the Moon?   9

Chapter Two

The gravity guys   28

Chapter Three

Trying to get to the Moon   36

Chapter Four

A rocket to the Moon   44

Chapter Five

The space race   67

Chapter Six

Blast off on your Moon mission   81

WHY BUILD A ROCKET?

That's one small step for a man, one giant leap for mankind.

On 20 July 1969, Neil Armstrong climbed in his bulky spacesuit down the ladder of his lunar module and took the first steps on the Moon. This was something that humans had dreamt about for thousands of years. His words are probably the most famous ever spoken (except everyone thinks that he actually said, 'That's one small step for man, one giant leap for mankind,' because the 'a' got lost in the radio transmission!).

This giant leap was possible because we finally managed to work out how to build a rocket that would get us to the moon. It took thousands of years and the work of the world's most brilliant scientists to build a rocket powerful enough to propel us out of Earth's atmosphere, and which could protect the brave astronauts inside from the deadly effects of space.

1   There is no air in space. If something makes a hole in your spacesuit or rocket, your eyeballs will be sucked out.

2   In space it can either be icy, deathly cold or so hot that you would fry without protection.

3   Space is a zero-gravity environment. This means that you are weightless, so it is difficult to move properly. (Astronauts who come back to Earth after a long time in space find that it's difficult for them to keep their balance.) Weightlessness also does horrible things to your body:

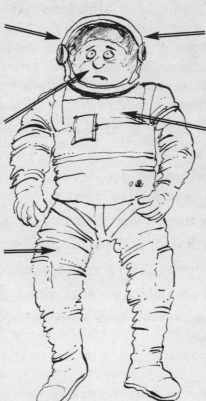

Your head moves around all over the place, which makes you feel dizzy and sick.

Your face gets puffy and swollen. (No rocket romance for you!) Your nose feels all plugged up because of the fluid in your head.

Your bones stop growing. (Astronauts who come back to Earth after spending alot of time in zero-gravity find that they break their bones easily.)

Blood collects in your head and chest because gravity isn't pulling it down.

Your heart shrinks because it doesn't have to work as hard as on Earth, and your muscles waste away for the same reason.

4   There are also asteroids, meteorites and bit of old satellites flying about; not to mention deadly radiation, and the Earth's atmosphere waiting to burn you up if you fall into it at the wrong time.

Besides all the dangers of travelling through space, it is very difficult to survive on the Moon. Your rocket has to carry all your food, fuel, clothing and equipment, as well as vast quantities of air to breathe.

In 1998, scientists were delighted to discover over 300 million tonnes of frozen water on the Moon. This makes it more likely that the long-term NASA objective of setting up a Moon base will happen in the future. But if you want to go to the Moon, you need to build a rocket to get you there. You also need to know what you are letting yourself in for. It's a trip only the bravest can make! This book will help. It will tell you all about:

* what the Moon is, how far away it is, and how it was made

* the silly ideas people used to have about the Moon and space travel

* how rockets were invented

* why it is so difficult for us to get to the Moon

* how to build your own spacesuit

* how to build a working rocket

* what to take with you when you travel to the Moon

CHAPTER ONE

WHAT IS THE MOON?

The Moon is a dusty ball of rock about a quarter of the size of Earth. It circles the Earth about once a month, in a path called an orbit. Because the Moon orbits around us, it is called our satellite.

The Moon is a dangerous place to be – there is no air to breathe and it can get as cold as -170°C at night. Brrr!

-170 °C?
That's even colder than our classroom in winter!

Humans have always wanted to go to the Moon, even when they didn't know what it was. And in the future, the Moon could be very useful to us. The American space agency NASA wants to set up a Moon base in the next century. This could be used as a launch pad for missions to other planets. We could also mine on the Moon, and use it to dump waste that would be harmful to get rid of here on Earth. Of course, the people living in the Moon base might not be too happy about that!

Here are some amazing Moon facts.

The Moon is 3,476 kilometres across.

The Moon is about 390,000 kilometres away from us.

There is no weather on the Moon (more about this later).

Lots of other planets in the solar system also have moons.

The Moon gives us light at night.

The Moon makes the seas move and gives us tides.

The Moon helped ancient people measure time.

Since civilisations began, people have stared up into the night sky and watched the Moon and the stars moving. But in ancient times people didn't know what they were. They came up with some amazing (and very stupid) explanations about what the Moon and stars are, why they move, and why the Moon changes shape.

Babylonian baloney

A Babylonian astronomer reckoned in around 1500 BC, 'The Moon and stars are where the gods live. The sky is just an arch stretching over the Earth. When we look at the Moon, it's like looking in through a god's window.'

But as well as having weird ideas, the Babylonians also correctly noticed that the Moon and stars move around in the sky.

The Babylonians thought the movements of the Moon and stars were messages from the gods, so they spent most nights staring up at them to try and read the messages. This started the ancient art of astrology. Even today, you can read in the newspaper what it means for your future when a star wanders across the sky a bit.

However, the Babylonians made very good maps showing exactly where the stars and Moon moved. It was because of this that later astronomers were able to work out that the Moon spins around planet Earth and that we spin around the Sun.

The Egyptian explanation ....

Other ancient peoples, such as the Egyptians, had different ideas to the Babylonians.

Of course, the Ancient Egyptians were wrong. A pig is not gobbling the Moon up every month! But you can see why they might have thought that, if you do the following experiment to see what happens to the Moon's shape.

Be a rocket scientist—
SEE HOW THE MOON SEEMS TO CHANGE SHAPE

WHAT YOU'LL NEED
- some paper and pens/pencils
- your eyes!

WHAT TO DO
1   Stand outside (or look out of your window) on a night when it isn't cloudy. Look at the Moon, draw what shape it is and write down the date. (If you can't see the Moon, write down that you can't see it, together with the date.)
2   Every night that you remember, look at the Moon and draw its shape.

WHAT HAPPENS?
Every month, the Moon changes shape lots of times. It starts off as a big circle — a full Moon (if you're superstitious, watch out for those werewolves!). Then it gets smaller and smaller, until it vanishes. Finally, it grows back into a full Moon.

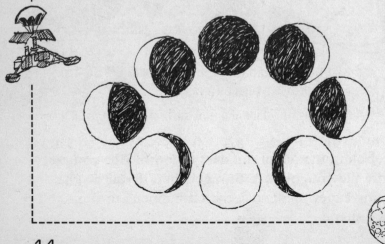

Mooning around ....

In fact, the Moon doesn't really change shape at all. It just *looks* as it's changing shape because of the way sunlight falls on it as it moves around us. The Moon reflects the light back at us like a dusty mirror. You can see what happens in this experiment.

Be a rocket scientist–
FIND OUT WHY THE MOON SEEMS TO CHANGE SHAPE

This experiment is best done in the dark.

WHAT YOU'LL NEED
- a small torch
- a tennis ball
- a dark room
- a chair that can spin round
- a friend

WHAT TO DO

1   Sit on the chair and hold the tennis ball in front of you. You are pretending to be a person standing on Earth and the tennis ball is a pretend Moon.

2   Ask your friend to turn off all the lights and turn on the torch. The torch is a pretend Sun.

3   Get your friend to shine the Sun torch on the tennis ball Moon.

4   Slowly spin round in your chair, holding the Moon in front of you. Watch what happens to the area of light on your Moon.

WHAT HAPPENS?
As you spin around, the Moon is sometimes between the torch and you, and you cannot see it. As it moves around, you can see more and more of it because more and more light falls on it. This is how the Moon appears to change shape.

Greek guesses ....

None of the ancient peoples were able to figure out that the Moon didn't really change shape. Even when the Ancient Greeks came along – and they were very clever – they couldn't make up their minds about why the Moon changed shape. (Perhaps this was because they didn't have swivel chairs to experiment with...) Some of them thought that the Moon was another big lump of rock like the Earth – which was the right idea – but others weren't convinced.

16

Other Greek scientists, such as Posidonius, had different ideas.

17

Anaximander, who lived in the 6th century BC, disagreed again.

Anaximander was a clever chap. He was one of the first people to work out that stars are actually great balls of fire. But he was wrong about the Moon being made of fire as well.

The arguments about the Moon were only solved when the telescope was invented and people could get a proper look at it. Everyone then agreed that the Moon shines because it reflects light from the Sun.

18

The Man in the Moon.........................

If you look at the full Moon, you'll see dark splodges
on it that look a bit like a face. People used to imagine
that there was a 'Man in the Moon'.

It was the work of Galileo Galilei, one of the greatest
ever scientists, which proved there wasn't a 'Man in
the Moon' after all.

Galileo gets a close-up
Italy, 1609

When Galileo Galilei heard about a new-fangled instrument called an optical tube (that's a telescope to you and me) he realized that it would be just the thing to help him find out more about the Moon. It took him years to work out how to build his own telescope, but when he finally succeeded, he found he could make things look 300 times bigger than they did before — just the thing to see what was really on the Moon.

Galileo was amazed!

When other astronomers heard about Galileo's discovery, they rushed to look at this marvellous new world. They all agreed with him. They began to draw maps of the Moon and even said that they could see trees and deformed Moon animals wandering around.

But Galileo was wrong. There are no beautiful seas on the Moon. The dark blobs he could see are really horrible dark craters. There are over 3 trillion of them, and the biggest one is about 295 kilometres wide and four kilometres deep!

The Moon is born
Italy, 1609

Most scientists think that the reason that there are no seas on the Moon and that it is pock-marked with huge craters is because the Moon used to be a bit of Earth, until a terrifying accident sent it spinning off into space. To see what happened, we have to go back in time to over 4 billion years ago…

Earth has just formed from a ball of red-hot gas, along with all the other planets in the solar system. There is no life here yet — which is a very good thing, because something devastating is about to happen. Looming in the distance and heading straight for us, is a lump of rock the size of the planet Mars.

When the lump of rock hits the Earth, the result is disastrous. Whole pieces of the Earth go spinning into space, along with the guilty planet that hit us.

The lumps of Earth rock are trapped in orbit around the Earth. Gradually, they bang into one another and stick together. After about 500 million years or so, the rocks cool and the Moon is born.

Meteorite mayhem ....

It's a good thing for us that the Moon was made, because we might not be here otherwise! When the solar system formed, there were millions of bits of rock floating around all over the place. Most of the time, these bits of rock just zoom around the Sun, not getting in anyone's way. But every so often, their paths cross with the orbit of one of the planets. The gravity of the planet helps to pull the rock towards it. This could cause a disaster if one hit Earth – even wiping us out completely! Luckily, the Moon orbits the Earth quite quickly and also has some gravity. This means that a rock set on impact with us is more likely to hit the Moon.

Scientists think that the Earth was hit by a massive meteorite 65 million years ago. It hurtled into the Earth's atmosphere and ended up falling on Mexico. It left a crater 200 kilometres across and threw clouds of poisonous dust and gas into the air which blocked out the sunlight and messed up the weather. Some scientists reckon that this is what might have made the dinosaurs extinct. If a really large meteorite hit the Earth today, it could kill all of us as well. So you can see how lucky it is that most meteorites hit the Moon and not us!

Smashed-up meteorites that have hit the Moon are scattered all over its surface as dusty rubble. Even today, the Moon is hit by 70 to 150 meteorites a year. Some of them weigh up to 1000 kilograms! If we are going to build a Moon base, we need to find some way of protecting it from falling meteorites. Scientists think that the best way might be to build the Moon base in underground tunnels.

Weathering meteorite showers ....

Even though there might be meteorites crashing down on your head, one reason why you might want to go to the Moon is because it never rains there – or snows, or hails, or hurricanes! Why? Because of the force of gravity. Gravity is what keeps your feet on the ground.

It also keeps the atmosphere on Earth from floating off into space. The Moon is smaller than the Earth and so it has less gravity – not enough to keep hold of an atmosphere. This means that you have to take your own air supply with you when you visit and hope that you don't run out!

But no air means no weather, too. Wind is moving air, and clouds only form when invisible water vapour in the air cools to form tiny droplets. If these droplets get big enough, then rain falls. On Earth this usually happens when air moves high into the atmosphere and cools down. You can make this happen at home.

Be a rocket scientist–
SEE WHY THERE IS
NO WEATHER ON THE MOON

WHAT YOU'LL NEED
- a glass jar with a wide neck
- a rubber glove with no holes
- a box of matches
- some water

WHAT TO DO

1   Cover the bottom of the jar with a thin layer of water.
2   Drop a lit match into the jar. (This makes smoke, which you'll need in order to see the cloud you are going to make.)
3   Put the rubber glove partly inside the jar, with the fingers hanging down inside. Stretch the top of the glove over the mouth of the jar to make a seal.

4   Put your hand into the glove and pull it up quickly,
    taking care that you don't pull the glove off the bottle.
    What happens?
5   Now repeat the experiment with no water in the bottle
    (but clean and dry the bottle and the glove first!). Does
    the same thing happen?

WHAT HAPPENS?
Some of the water you have put in the jar evaporates and turns
into water vapour. When you pull the glove up, you make the
air in the jar spread out. This makes it cool down. You make a
cloud in the bottle! When there is no water in the bottle, no
cloud forms. This is why there is no rain on the Moon.

CHAPTER TWO

THE GRAVITY GUYS

After maps had been drawn of the amazing Moon, covered with beautiful seas with strange names, people were very keen to go and visit. But this was easier said than done. The Moon is thousands of kilometres away through the deadly vacuum of space (with not a service station in sight...).

The main problem is getting off the Earth in the first place! Gravity holds us towards the Earth so strongly that it takes enormous force to get anything into space. If your rocket is just a little too puny, you'll be pulled back to Earth and squashed into tiny pieces.

Most of our knowledge about gravity was worked out by three scientists. The first to puzzle about why things are pulled down to the ground was an Ancient Greek (yes, another one!) called Aristotle.

Everything is made up of earth, water, fire or air! Each of these things has a place where it likes to be. So, a stone falls because it has earth in it, and earth belongs on the ground. Oww!

This may sound really silly to us nowadays, but people believed this idea for nearly 1900 years. Then in Italy in 1586, Simon Stevinus came along and did a very famous experiment. (Well, he said it was an experiment, but it was probably an accident when he was bumped from behind by a tourist.) Simon Stevinus was up a tower when he dropped the two things he was holding and they fell over the edge. We don't know what these things were. But we do know that even though they had different weights, they hit the ground at the same time!

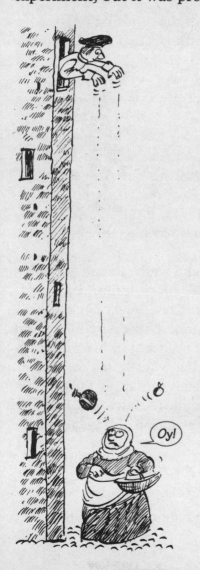

Oy!

Remember Galileo, the world's greatest scientist? Well, he couldn't bear for someone to discover something he didn't know about. He repeated Simon's experiment and also started rolling balls down slopes to see what happened to them. He said that if something fell, it speeded up. But even he couldn't explain why. In the end, he gave up in disgust.

Newton's news ....

The top gravity guy was Isaac Newton.

It's 1665, the year of the Black Death. People all over Europe are developing horrible black lumps on their bodies and dropping dead like flies. Yuck! Isaac has been sent home from Cambridge University to try and avoid the plague. One day he is sitting in his garden at Woolsthorpe Manor, wondering what keeps the Moon going round the Earth. Suddenly, an apple falls to the ground, and he has a brilliant idea. Newton called his idea the Universal Law of Gravitation. It explained lots of things, including:

- ● why heavy things fall on your toes
- ● why the seas move in tides every day
- ● why the Moon doesn't shoot off into space.

His idea was that...

30

The Moon circles the Earth because of gravity! It's the same force that pulls the apple to the ground.

Be a rocket scientist—
SEE HOW GRAVITY MAKES THE MOON ORBIT EARTH

Although the Earth's gravity pulls the Moon towards it, the Moon doesn't hit the Earth because it is moving so quickly. The speed of the Moon keeps it moving in a circular orbit. You can see how this works in a very simple experiment.

WHAT YOU'LL NEED
- a long piece of string
- a ball of plasticine about the size of a marble
- some outside space

WHAT TO DO

1 The plasticine ball is your Moon and the string is pretend gravity. Attach the plasticine ball to the end of your piece of string.

2 Stand with your piece of string in your hand and spin around. You are the Earth spinning.

3 Watch what happens to the plasticine Moon. Then try spinning the plasticine Moon faster and slower. What happens?

4 Make sure no one is around and let go of the Moon. What happens?

What on earth is going on?

WHAT HAPPENS?

The plasticine Moon wants to go off in a straight line, yet it can't. But it doesn't get any closer to you, because it is moving very fast.

If you let go of the string, the plasticine shoots off in a straight line. Without gravity, this is what would happen to the Moon: it would shoot off in a straight line and disappear into space.

Gravity is also what keeps the Earth in orbit around the Sun.

All washed up! ....

Newton could also explain why the seas move up and down every day. It's because the pull of the Moon's gravity on the seas creates bulges, so that the sea level is higher in some places than in others.

Where's the sea gone then?

Be a rocket scientist—
SEE HOW GRAVITY MOVES THE SEA

Gravity is a pulling force. It's impossible for you to create gravity yourself, but you can see how gravity pulls water towards the Moon by creating another pulling force called electrostatic attraction. Electrostatic attraction happens when something has an electric charge.

WHAT YOU'LL NEED
- a running tap
- a balloon
- a woolly jumper or a soft duster

WHAT TO DO
1 Blow up your balloon. This is going to be your Moon.
2 Now give your balloon an electric charge by rubbing it quickly (and carefully, so that it doesn't pop!) against the jumper or the duster.
3 Turn your tap on and hold the balloon close to the water. What happens?

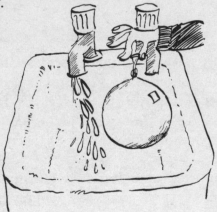

WHAT HAPPENS?
The water moves towards the balloon! This is similar to what happens when gravity from the Moon pulls on the seas.

Planet power ....

When Newton said that everything had gravity, he meant everything. Even you have gravity!

The problem is that gravity is a very puny force, and you're not big enough to have enough gravity to pull things towards you. Sorry! It's only when something is as big as a moon or a planet that we start to feel the gravitational force.

But even though gravity is a puny force, Earth is so large that we can't beat its gravitational pull by ourselves. To get to the Moon, we need something that can defeat the force of gravity and fly for thousands of kilometres without needing to refuel – something that people have been trying to find for thousands of years...

TRYING TO GET TO THE MOON

Ever since the Ancient Greeks realized that the Moon was not a lump of green cheese but a big lump of rock, people have dreamed of getting there. Before this century, it was impossible to succeed, because nobody had even figured out how to get off the ground and stay up in the air for very long! But that didn't put them off. People still came up with lots of amazing ideas for how they might get there and what would happen when they did!

Traveller's tales....................................

The first stories about travelling to the Moon were written by the Ancient Greek (yes, I know – yet another one!) Lucian in 160 AD. He had two ways of getting there: firstly, being snatched up by a whirlwind; and secondly, by fastening a vulture's wing to one shoulder and an eagle's wing to the other, then flying there.

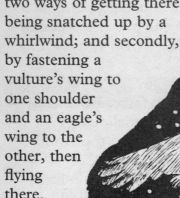

Spaceships? Pah! Who needs them? Eat your heart out, Captain Kirk!

And our hero didn't stop when he got to the Moon!
He also travelled to Venus and some of the stars!

Spaced out ....

After Lucian's tales, no more space travel stories were
written for hundreds of years. This was mainly
because the Christian church didn't want anybody
writing about different worlds. But when Lucian's
stories were published again in the 17th century, it
inspired everyone to have a go.

A book by Johannes Kepler was published in 1634,
after he had died. Kepler was a very famous
astronomer, and so his book was less silly than
Lucian's.

What he got right:	People travelling into space feel weightless and have problems breathing.
	Night on the Moon lasts for 15 to 16 days.
What he got wrong:	The Moon is full of snake-like animals and plants. Every day they grow to huge sizes and when the Sun goes down they hide underground or die!

Bishops blast off into space.................

Two books were written in 1638 by bishops. *The Man in the Moone* was written by Francis Godwin. He claimed that people could get to the Moon by tying themselves to wild swans.

Bishop John Wilkins' book was called *The Discovery of a World in the Moone.*

What he got right: People are weightless in space.

What he got wrong: People in space do not need food or sleep.
People can get to the Moon in a flying chariot.

Astronauts ahoy! ....

Soon everyone was trying to design a spaceship to take them to the Moon. In 1650, the famous Frenchman Cyrano de Bergerac (of big-nose fame!) came up with three ideas.

Rocket man ....

People may have laughed at these ideas, but Cyrano had indeed hit on the right one – rockets! It's the Earth's gravity that makes it so difficult to get to the Moon. Gravity is useful for holding us down on the ground, but it's hard to beat. To escape from its clutches completely, you need to reach a speed of over 10 kilometres per second! Rockets are the only thing we have that can beat the force of gravity and break out of the Earth's atmosphere. Even the modern Space Shuttle uses rockets to launch it into space.

How does a rocket work? ......

You might think that because rockets are powerful enough to take a metal tin full of humans and equipment to the Moon and back, they must be very complicated. In fact, they're so simple, a baby could understand how they work.

The rocket is a long tube. The rocket fuel burns inside the tube and gives off very hot gases. There is a hole at the end of the rocket to let the hot gases escape. As the gas shoots out, the rocket takes off.

41

Be a rocket scientist—
SEE HOW A ROCKET WORKS

WHAT YOU'LL NEED
- a balloon

WHAT TO DO

1 Blow up the balloon.
2 Let go of it!

PHWAAARGH!

WHAT HAPPENS?

The air in the balloon rushes out of the hole at the end and pushes the balloon along. This is just how a rocket moves.

Over the years, people have come up with many different ways to use the rocket – some very strange, some very dangerous, some useful and some simply fun…

CHAPTER FOUR

A ROCKET TO THE MOON

Nobody really knows for sure when rockets were first invented, but most people think that the Chinese invented them around 1000 AD. They found them very useful as weapons…

The Mad History of Rockets

Part I: Kai-fung-fu, China; 1232 AD

Kai-fung-fu is a Chinese town in terror. Hordes of Mongol horsemen have surrounded the town and are just waiting for their chance to attack. The brave soldiers defending this town are outnumbered… Oh no! The Mongols are coming into attack!

But what's this? The Mongols are being driven back by what looks like arrows of fire! I don't believe it! They've attached little rockets to their arrows! The arrows are zooming around at high speed and exploding just like fireworks!

The Mongols are wetting themselves! To make things worse, they're having gunpowder bombs dropped on their heads as well. They're in retreat! The rocket arrows have saved the day!

The Mad History of Rockets

Part II:

China, 1420

"Wan Hu, a well-known official, has decided to see if he can use rockets to fly. He's built an amazing flying machine out of two kites with a seat fastened underneath. His flying machine is going to be powered by 47 — yes, that's 47 — rockets! 47 assistants are standing by, ready to light each of the rockets at the same time."

"Wan Hu is climbing into his seat. His assistants are getting ready. The tension is unbearable... Oh! He's given the signal! The assistants are rushing in with their torches..."

"Oh my goodness! What an explosion!"

And Wan Hu was never seen again. This story was probably why people didn't try using rockets to fly again for a long time.

Rockets are all the rage! ....

In the 1800s, bombarding Napoleon with rockets saved England from being invaded by the French. Apart from that, people thought rockets weren't much use for anything except Bonfire Night displays. But some scientists and inventors were still impressed with the speed of rockets and thought there must be something else they could do with them. They came up with some incredible rocket inventions, like:

- A rocket plane (which didn't fly)
- Getting rid of storm clouds by firing rockets into them
- Lifting spy cameras into the sky on rockets and bringing them back down by parachute (this worked quite well)
- Rocket-propelled cars...
- ...and mail delivery by rocket.

I thought my new mail delivery idea would really take off!

But rockets were soon to have their day. At the beginning of the 20th century, a Swedish rocket scientist called Wilhelm Unge announced to the world that he had developed an 'aerial torpedo'. He had improved the puny old war rockets that could only fly for a couple of kilometres by powering them with nitroglycerine. (This is the stuff that dynamite is made of, so you can imagine how far and fast they flew!) He thought that they would be useful for shooting down any hot air balloons that happened to sail over his back garden. The Germans agreed with him and bought a load to experiment with. They came in very useful during the war, when hot-air balloons were used to try to see behind enemy lines.

49

World War II saw researchers from all the countries fighting amongst themselves to see who could make the most powerful rocket weapons. The German scientists started the war in the lead with a rocket called the Nebelwerfer. The British and US troops called it the 'Screaming Meemie', because of the dreadful screeching noise it made as it came into land. The Americans answered back with the bazooka – a hand-held rocket launcher. The Germans were taken completely by surprise when it was used to blast into their armoured tanks! But they soon developed their own bazooka, which they called the 'Tank Terror'.

However, the most important rockets in World War II were huge weapons that flew for hundreds of kilometres before flattening their target. The Germans had the V2 rocket, which was one of the most terrifying weapons of the war. If your grandparents are alive, they may remember these. Thousands fell on England during the war, causing enormous damage.

After World War II, some scientists realized that if a rocket could fly along for 200 kilometres, then it should be able to fly up 200 kilometres as well. Designing a rocket that could do this and take us to the Moon was mainly the work of four people...

The Rocket Researchers

Part I: America, 1926

The American space scientist Robert Goddard got the rocket bug when he was only 16 and reading the novel *War of the Worlds*, where horrible Martians invade Earth and blast everyone to pieces. He began to dream of trying to find a way to get to Mars himself.

In 1908, Goddard started work experimenting on rockets and was the first person to show that a rocket could fly when there was no air, just like in space.

Goddard also changed the fuel that his rockets used. Early rockets used solid fuel. But Goddard knew that to get to the Moon, an enormous amount of fuel would be needed. And there would be a big problem in space because there is no air. Fuel in cars and aeroplanes needs oxygen from the air to burn properly, but fuel in rockets needs to have its own oxygen supply, otherwise the rocket will fizzle out and splutter back to Earth. Goddard made an important decision. To get to the Moon, rockets needed to carry not solid fuel, not even gas fuel, but liquid fuel. And he was right. In 1926, he launched the world's first liquid-powered rocket from his Aunt Effie's farm. It only just got off the ground, but that didn't matter — the point was that it worked.

Why can't the fuel be a gas?.................

A rocket needs to burn an immense amount of fuel to get into space. The molecules in a gas are much further apart than they are in a liquid. This means that if you use liquid fuel, you pack more molecules in the same space than you would if you stored it as gas.

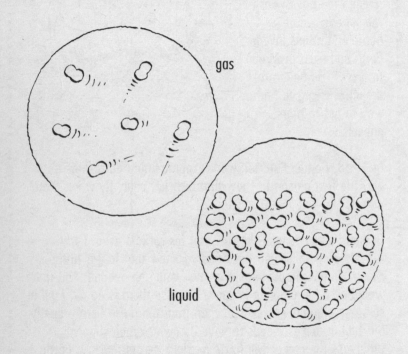

gas

liquid

In the first rockets that got to the Moon, the fuel was liquid hydrogen and liquid oxygen. This burns very easily and makes water as a waste product. The liquid hydrogen needs to be kept in a separate fuel tank, so that it doesn't burn until you want it to.

The inside of a
liquid-fuel rocket
looks like this.

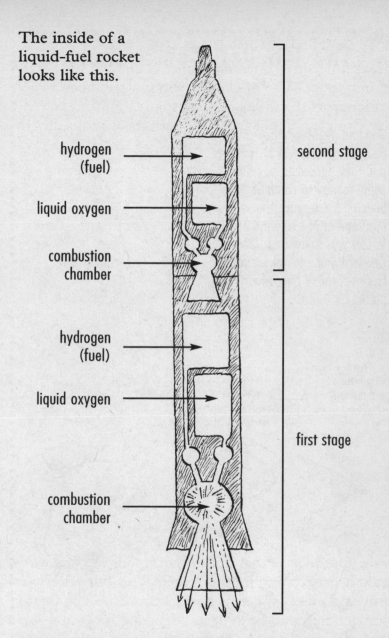

hydrogen
(fuel)

liquid oxygen

combustion
chamber

second stage

hydrogen
(fuel)

liquid oxygen

first stage

combustion
chamber

The liquid oxygen and hydrogen are pumped into a
special combustion chamber, where they burn.

The Rocket Researchers

Part I, continued:

America, 1930s

Goddard eventually got some people interested in his rockets and they agreed to pay him some money to continue building them — to the amusement of everyone else! Robert was known as 'Moony' Goddard and each of his rocket launches made him a laughing-stock...

That thing'll never get to the Moon!

Yeah — it's got as much chance as the eagles' wings idea!

54

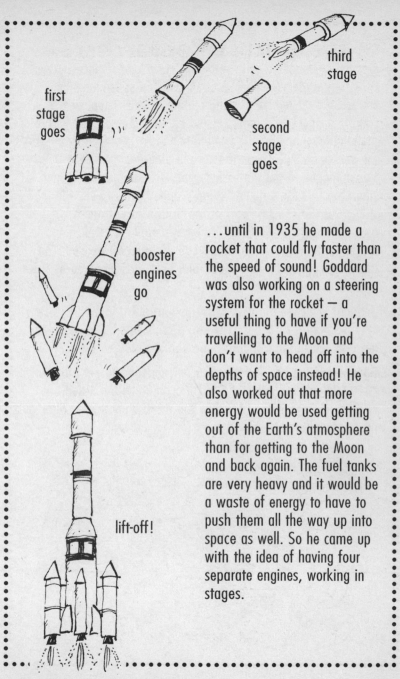

first
stage
goes

third
stage

second
stage
goes

booster
engines
go

lift-off!

...until in 1935 he made a rocket that could fly faster than the speed of sound! Goddard was also working on a steering system for the rocket — a useful thing to have if you're travelling to the Moon and don't want to head off into the depths of space instead! He also worked out that more energy would be used getting out of the Earth's atmosphere than for getting to the Moon and back again. The fuel tanks are very heavy and it would be a waste of energy to have to push them all the way up into space as well. So he came up with the idea of having four separate engines, working in stages.

This idea was used for the Apollo spaceships — the spaceships that did eventually reach the Moon. Each Apollo spaceship was carried by a rocket called Saturn V which was bigger than a 10-storey block of flats and made up half of the weight of the rocket. The fuel in its tanks lasted for only 30 seconds before the stage dropped off the bottom of the rocket. (Watch out for the people below!) Then the second stage engines took over. This managed to get the rocket over 180 kilometres up, and when the fuel ran out, this stage dropped off as well. The third stage was the smallest part of the Saturn rocket and this managed to get the rocket into Earth's orbit. After blasting the rocket towards the Moon, this stage dropped off as well. The rest of the journey to the Moon and back was powered by the engines in the spaceship itself.

Goddard launched the first liquid-fuelled rocket in 1926. It flew only 56 metres at about 100 km/h. This was far too slow to get into space, but Goddard knew that it could be done.

Goddard carried on, and in 1935 he managed to get a rocket to go 1.6 kilometres into the sky. Unfortunately, the Americans were more interested in building the atom bomb at the time, so they ignored him.

Revolutionary rocket design ....

There were other important changes to make to rocket design before rockets could fly to the Moon and back. First, the way that the hot gas is pushed out of the rocket changes how fast it can go. Rockets all have nozzles at the bottom, shaped like an upside-down funnel.

They have this because they make the rockets more powerful. Rockets that can get into space need very large nozzles to reach supersonic speeds (speeds that are faster than the speed of sound).

Be a rocket scientist–
FIND THE BEST NOZZLE
FOR YOUR ROCKET

Oi! What are you doing?

You can experiment to see how changing the shape of a nozzle makes your rocket go further.

WHAT YOU'LL NEED

- a long balloon
- a room
- a straw
- a pair of scissors
- the lid of a washing-up liquid bottle
- a long piece of thread
- sellotape
- a peg
- some card or stiff paper

WHAT TO DO

1   Tape the thread to the wall at one side of a room.
2   Cut a length of straw about 10-15 centimetres long and thread the straw onto the thread.
3   Tape the other end of the thread to the opposite wall.

Blow up the balloon and use the peg to seal it until you are ready to fire your rocket.

5   Tape your rocket balloon (with the peg still sealing it) to the straw.

6   Now launch your rocket by taking off the peg. See how far across the room it goes and how fast.

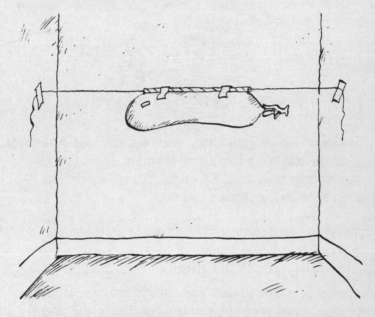

7   Take your rocket off the string and blow it up again. In the mouth of the balloon, put the nozzle from the washing-up bottle.

8   Tape your balloon to the straw again and launch the rocket once more. Time how fast it goes.

9   Now make a cone-shaped nozzle out of the card.

10 Blow up the balloon again and put the nozzle on the end. Launch this rocket and time how fast it goes across the room.

The rocket balloon goes fastest when the air comes out through a narrow hole into a funnel-shaped nozzle. This is how all rockets have to be built. (Of course, you can try and find an even better nozzle shape if you wish!)

Balancing your booster...........................

A rocket is more than a tube with nozzles. If you launched your rocket now it would take off and fly all over the place, just as if you blew up a balloon and let go of it. That's not what you want at all. The rocket has to fly straight up into the air. You need something to stabilize the rocket and keep it on a steady course.

For hundreds of years, people used large sticks to balance their rockets out. In the 1700s, the Indian army used rockets stabilized by three-metre-long bamboo poles as weapons. The bamboo pole was almost as deadly as the rocket itself.

If you look at rocket fireworks you'll see that they still use sticks to make them run in a straight line. However, there are two main reasons why you can't use a big stick to stabilize a rocket to take you to the Moon.

1 Your rocket has to be about 110 metres high to carry enough fuel to get you into space. It would be very hard finding a stick that big!

2 The rocket goes so fast through the air as it takes off that it would be very difficult to get a stick to stay stuck on. It would just blow off – even with superglue.

In the 1800s, William Hale, an English scientist, found a way of building war rockets without the guide-stick. He stuck flaps in the nozzle, called vanes. This made the rocket fly in a straight line, but it also made it spin around as it flew!

In modern rockets, like the ones you'll fly to the Moon, the vanes are on the outside of the rocket. They are controlled by a gyroscope – a fast-spinning wheel that you can't tilt, however hard you try. The gyroscope keeps the vanes in the position where the rocket is stabilized.

Be a rocket scientist—
INVESTIGATE GYROSCOPES

WHAT YOU'LL NEED
- a bicycle wheel
- a friend
- two pairs of thick gloves (gardening ones are ideal)

WHAT TO DO

1   Put on the gloves and hold the wheel in both hands by the axle.
2   Try tilting the wheel from one side to the other. How easy is it?
3   Hold the wheel upright again and ask your friend to put their gloves on.
4   While you hold the wheel, your friend can spin it by pulling down on the tyre.
5   When the wheel is spinning quite quickly, try to tilt the wheel again.

WHAT HAPPENS
When the wheel is still, it is very easy to tilt it to one side or another. When the wheel is spinning, it is much harder to tilt. The heavier the wheel and the faster it is spinning, the harder it is to tilt. This is how the gyroscope in a rocket works. It spins so quickly that it is very difficult to tilt over. This keeps the rocket moving in a straight line.

The Rocket Researchers

Part II:

Russia, 1890s–1930s

Besides Goddard, another important rocket scientist was a Russian called Konstantin Tsiolkovsky. Konstantin had a hard life. At the age of nine he caught scarlet fever and became deaf. Then when he was a student in Moscow he had to teach himself and ate only stale bread so that he could buy books. He spent most of his life as a high school teacher and had a little basement where he could do his experiments in his spare time.

Will you get this thing out of my living room!

Konstantin was obsessed with getting humans to fly and into space. He built a wind tunnel out of odd bits and pieces of material to test the design of aircraft and rockets. He was also interested in how we would talk to alien creatures when we did get to other planets! More importantly, he agreed with Goddard that rockets should have liquid fuel. He also suggested satellites orbiting the Earth and space stations inbetween each of the planets. He died in 1935, so you can see how far ahead of his time he was — but most of his work was sadly ignored.

The Rocket Researchers

Part III:

Austria and Hungary, 1920s–1930s

The third important rocket scientist was Hermann Oberth, who came from Transylvania. He wrote a book about rockets which was published in Germany in 1923 – although he had to pay for it to be published himself as it was rejected by the university he had sent it to. Oberth also sent a design for a long-range, liquid-fuelled rocket to the War Ministry, who also laughed at his idea and said it was nothing but a fantasy!

Scientists and engineers may have ignored Oberth's work, but some writers loved it and set up a space travel society. This society messed about with loads of rockets but didn't have much success. This could have been because at this time, Oberth didn't really know how to build a rocket. In 1928 he was asked to build a rocket for a space film. Unfortunately, it was a complete failure...

Later on, Hermann did build some working rockets. He also managed to work out the very complicated sums that showed how fast a rocket would have to fly to escape from Earth's gravity. He also found out how to pretend he was weightless — a useful thing to try out before you go into space! In 1940, Hermann became a German citizen and went to work for his former assistant (now his boss) Wernher von Braun.

 # The Rocket Researchers

Part IV:

Germany, 1930s

Wernher von Braun was one of the most important rocket researchers. He became interested in rockets as a child, when he read Hermann's book on space and couldn't understand the maths. He decided to work hard until he was the best in the class. Soon after he left school, he joined a space travel society and helped Hermann in his spare time. By the time World War II started, Wernher was working on developing very powerful and deadly rockets. The most famous rocket he worked on was the V-2. By the time the war ended, the Germans knew more about building long-range rockets than any other country on Earth!

During the war, there was no time to test out whether a V-2 could fly into space. But at the end of the war, when the whole of Wernher's rocket team surrendered to the Americans (who had almost no knowledge of building very powerful rockets), the Americans immediately put Wernher onto a missile building programme. At the same time, the Russians took over most of the German rocket-building factories. The race for space had started!

CHAPTER FIVE

THE SPACE RACE

After the war, scientists knew that rockets could be fired into space. The work of all the rocket researchers had shown that. But a rocket had yet to be built that was large enough to carry enormous amounts of fuel plus equipment, water and air for any people that would get into space. The Americans had the knowledge of Wernher and his crew. The Russians also had some good scientists and all the rocket building equipment. Who would be the first to win the race? It took 12 years to find out and it proved to be the most exciting race in the history of the world!

Here we are on planet Earth, where the backward species that call themselves humans are finally trying to get into space, only 10,000 years after us! There are two teams – the Americans and the Russians. For some reason they want to try and get to this dusty lump of rock with nothing on it called the Moon. (They should try and visit the planet Zarg, which is much more interesting!)

To make things more difficult, and to try and stop them cheating, the teams are separated by a screen called the Iron Curtain. This means they can't see what the other side are doing until their rockets are in space! Oh, and they're off...

The Americans take off at high speed. They want to catch up with what the Germans managed to do with the V-2. Oh! They've got a rocket 400 kilometres into space! Wonderful! Now they're trying to find out if they can put a nuclear bomb on a rocket... They can! But people aren't impressed — they're very worried about the possibility of nuclear war, and this forces the Americans to slow down. Can the Russians catch them up?

Yes they can! The Russians have got a satellite called Sputnik I to go around in Earth's orbit.

The Americans are shocked. They don't know what to do...

And it gets worse for them. The Russians have blasted another satellite up, this time with a living four-legged creature inside – a dog! And the dog has survived in space! (Unfortunately the poor thing was killed when the rocket fell back down to Earth and burnt up.)

Now the Americans are running faster. They've finally got a satellite into space. It sends back pictures that show that the Earth is slightly pear-shaped.

The Russians just laugh. They've launched Lunik I at the Moon. The Americans hold their breath... but, phew! Lunik misses and goes into orbit around the Sun. The Russians claim that this is the first artificial, planet and call it Dream. (Ha! They haven't seen the artificial planet my people made – a thousand times bigger!)

The Americans can only sulk and stare in disbelief as the Russians try again. Lunik II crash-lands on the Moon. This proves that rockets can get there! And now this is getting silly. The Russians launch Lunik III and they get it to go around the Moon. It sends back pictures of the side of the Moon that humans have never seen. (Though if they wanted to know what it looked like, they could have asked us!) But where are the Americans? They're getting seriously left behind...

And the Russians are pulling ahead even more. They've blasted a 5-tonne rocket into space with a man called Yuri Gagarin inside. What a triumph! The Russians have got the first man into space. Now the Americans are really worried. They've got to do something.

The Americans reply by blasting Alan Shepard into space. Now the race might get interesting. The Americans try again and get a man into orbit for 16 minutes.

The Russians just sneer and thumb their noses. They send a man into orbit for 25.6 hours. He goes around the Earth 17 times. The Americans are trying very hard, but they just can't seem to do as well as the Russians. They've got a man into orbit for only three times around the Earth. It looks like the Russians are going to win the race.

Now both runners are trying to see if humans can survive in space long enough to get to the Moon and back. The Americans get Gordon Cooper to stay up there for 34 hours. But the Russians are miles ahead – they've got a woman in space and she's been up there for 78 hours! Surely this is enough to let them win the race!

And this is even more amazing! The Russians have got a man to wander about in space in just his spacesuit – for 20 minutes!

But the Americans are making another superhuman effort. They manage to get a spaceship into space with two men in it – and keep them there for 190 hours. And they've made a clever backpack thing that pushes you around when you get out of your rocket. Oh dear, the Russians appear to be slowing down.

Hi!

But the Americans were getting too confident. The Russian spaceship Luna IX has landed on the Moon safely! There was no one in it, but it looks as if it's all over for the Americans... Or is it? The Americans also get a spaceship to land on the Moon. It sends back lots of pretty pictures. Then the Russians send another spaceship to the Moon. It sends back information about the soil. And it looks like the Russians are also getting interested in Venus. They've sent a spaceship to Venus – and it's landed!

But now both sides have had terrible accidents. The Americans were testing a spaceship and it's burst into flames. The three astronauts inside have died. And the Russians have lost a cosmonaut. He was trying to get back into the Earth's atmosphere from orbit and his parachute lines became tangled up. He crashed to the Earth.

Moon walking ....

So why didn't the Americans or Russians send people to the Moon as soon as they knew a rocket could get that far?

Well, at the time, nobody knew what effects being in space for a long time would have on astronauts. They also didn't know if the Moon was safe to land on. This is why they had to land unmanned spaceships on the Moon. Scientists tried to find out with robots and computers whether the soil was safe to walk on, if the spaceship would just sink into the soil when it landed, and where the safest place to land was. There was also a very tiny chance that there were living creatures on the Moon – and they may not have been too happy about us landing on it!

Besides, space is very very dangerous for humans. Spaceships had to be designed that could carry two or three astronauts to the Moon and back, along with enough air, water and food to keep them alive.

This wasn't easy. It meant that the rockets had to be very big and even heavier, and so they had to be more powerful to get into space. However, once scientists had managed to land a few spaceships on the Moon safely, they thought it should be possible to get them back home, too.

The disasters that struck both teams set back the race for space. The American mission was slowed down by a year and the Russian one by two years. This gave the Americans the head start they needed.

And so the race continued...

Well, both teams have rested for a while and now it's all go again! And now the Americans seem to be in the lead. They get two more spaceships onto the Moon. They test the soil and the scientists work out that it is safe to walk on! But the spaceships that land have to stay there. I know the humans are stupid, but I can't imagine anyone volunteering to go to the Moon and never come back! What they need is to get a spaceship to go to the Moon and back. Can they do it?

Yes! The Russians have done it! Their spaceship Zond 5 has travelled around the Moon and come back to Earth... But what's this? The Americans pull ahead again! Saturn V has taken three astronauts around the Moon and brought them back to Earth safely!

Where are the Russians now? They're testing out spaceships that can link up in space. They seem to have forgotten about the Moon. And the Americans have won! They've got two men on the Moon! The race is over!

Giving up and going home ....

The Russians never did land people on the Moon.
The Americans landed people on the Moon six times,
the last time in 1972. Since then, nothing has
happened. All that there is to prove we have ever been
there is the equipment we left behind us. All that
effort seems to have been for nothing. Why?

Well, the Americans stopped going to the Moon
because it was too expensive. Instead, NASA has
concentrated on exploring other planets by sending
remote controlled probes through the solar system.
We have discovered that Venus has a temperature of
900°C and so would not be a very nice place to visit.
We also know that there are no Martians on Mars,
and that Uranus and Neptune have rings, as well as
Saturn. NASA has also been putting money into
developing reusable spaceships like the Space Shuttle,
which started flying in 1981. Because this can be used
over 100 times and a rocket can only be
used once, it has meant that missions into
space are cheaper. However, the Space
Shuttle was designed to carry satellites
and parts of space stations
into orbit. The Space Shuttle
cannot fly to the Moon and
it couldn't land on the rocky
surface. A newly-designed
reusable rocket
will be
needed
for that.

NASA
DESIGN
DEPT.

Now that scientists have discovered frozen water on the Moon – and if we can crack the problem of designing a reusable rocket powerful enough to reach the Moon – it seems more likely that we will one day be able to set up a Moon base. We now know that water will not have to be carried up there for people to drink and to grow food with. And water could be used as a fuel for spaceships because it can be split up into oxygen and hydrogen. Building a Moon base would mean that we can use the Moon as a stepping stone to get to the other planets that we want to explore, like Mars. But if you want to go there, you'll have to get in training!

CHAPTER SIX

BLAST OFF ON YOUR MOON MISSION

Right! Are you ready to get going to the Moon?

Step 1

To travel to the Moon, you first have to satisfy the requirements for astronaut training. How do you match up to the astronaut checklist for the very first Moon missions?

ASTRONAUT CHECKLIST, AD1968
- MUST BE LESS THAN 40 YEARS OLD
- MUST BE NO TALLER THAN 5 FEET 11 INCHES
- MUST BE IN EXCELLENT PHYSICAL CONDITION
- MUST HAVE AN ENGINEERING DEGREE
- MUST HAVE FLOWN A PLANE FOR 1500 HOURS (PREFERABLY A HIGH-SPEED JET)
- MUST **NOT** BE A WOMAN (ONLY THE **R**USSIANS GOT A WOMAN INTO SPACE)

How are you doing so far? If you've failed that test, never mind. Being an astronaut nowadays is a bit easier (as long as you don't want to be the pilot). You need to be:

If you want to be a pilot, you'd have to fly a jet aircraft for over a thousand hours. (The RAF would probably not appreciate you borrowing one of their planes for that long.) And if that's not enough, all astronauts get extra training in meterology, guidance and navigation, astronomy, physics and computer science. (Now do you see why your teacher keeps bugging you about your homework?) If it all sounds too difficult, don't give up! Perhaps you might be able to convince an astronaut training centre that you're a child genius and that your school report is really a degree certificate...

The first part of your training will be zero-gravity. This is difficult on Earth, but it can be done. A special aircraft is flown in a curve. The people inside feel weightless for up to half a minute, and float around.

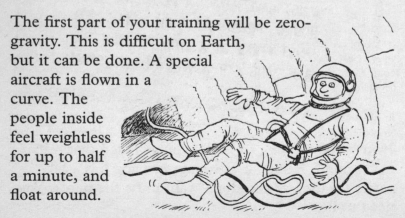

You'll also be doing a lot of training underwater, because you're more floaty there. (If you want to try this in the local swimming pool, don't wear a spacesuit or you'll get funny looks.)

Once you've got through zero-gravity training, you'll need to get kitted out.

Step 2 ....

If you want to walk on the Moon you'll need a spacesuit – and you can't buy them in shops. Here's what you need to build your own.

Cool water running through tubes in your underwear to stop you getting all hot and sweaty. Otherwise your visor would steam up and you wouldn't be able to see where you were going!

Clothes pumped full of air. This protects you from the difference in air pressure you find on the Moon, otherwise you'd get dizzy and fall over. But it does have to be jointed.

Just in case you get dizzy and fall over, cover your suit with a protective covering that's tough and won't rip. (If it does, you're in big trouble!)

The original Moon astronauts had velcro attached to the inside of their visor so that they could scratch their nose if it was itchy!

This box thing is called a Portable Life Support System and it carries oxygen. Hoses carry the oxygen through to your suit. They also take away carbon dioxide from you breathing out (and methane from your farts).

Boots, gloves and a helmet. These must be attached to your spacesuit so that it is airtight. The visor on the helmet has a silvery coating to protect you from the Sun's rays.

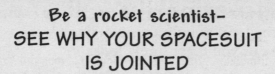

Be a rocket scientist–
SEE WHY YOUR SPACESUIT
IS JOINTED

Your spacesuit needs to be pumped up with air, but this can make moving around very difficult. So your spacesuit has to be jointed. You can see why in this experiment.

WHAT YOU'LL NEED
- two long thin balloons
- some elastic bands

WHAT TO DO
1. Blow one balloon up very hard.
2. Blow the other balloon up equally, but slip two or three elastic bands on to it to make it look like a string of sausages.
3. Try and bend each balloon, as if they were arms picking something up.

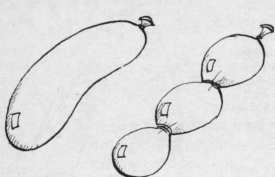

WHAT HAPPENS?
The balloon that is jointed bends much more easily than the one that isn't.

Answering the call of nature

Here's a problem. You're on the Moon, jumping around, and suddenly you need to go to the toilet. What do you do?

A   Take off your trousers and find a rock to hide behind?

B   Cross your legs and try to hold on until you get back to your spaceship?

C   Wet yourself?

The answer is C! Well, not exactly. But you can't take your trousers off on the Moon – you'd freeze and all of the air would be sucked out of your spacesuit. (Nasty!) So, before you put on your spacesuit, you have to wear a nappy! (Don't worry, all astronauts on the Moon hate wearing them.)

Besides the spacesuit that you wear in space or on the Moon, you need another one for take off and landing. This one is bright orange, in case something goes wrong and you need to be seen by emergency services. It's a very special suit because it squeezes your legs. Without this suit, you would pass out when you took off or landed. The speeds you are moving at make the blood in your body behave in a very strange way. This suit keeps most of the blood where it should be – in the top of your body where it can get to your brain, not making your ankles swell up.

Step 3 ....

So you're kitted out with the right clothing. Now all you need is a rocket.

By now, you should know enough to be able to build a full-size Moon rocket. But if there isn't enough room for one in your back garden, you can try building this water-powered rocket out of washing-up bottles.

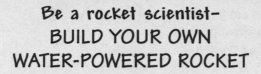

Be a rocket scientist—
BUILD YOUR OWN
WATER-POWERED ROCKET

WHAT YOU'LL NEED
- 2 squeezy washing-up liquid bottles
- strong scissors
- a bicycle pump or foot pump with an adapter for blowing up footballs
- a launch pad made from a sheet of plywood or cardboard leant against something

WHAT TO DO
1. Take the nozzles of the bottles and wash everything. Leave them to dry.
2. Cut the top and bottom off one bottle. Keep the top piece, with its nozzle.

3. Cut the rest of the bottle up its side and flatten it out to make a sheet of plastic.

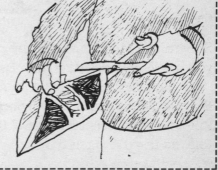

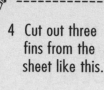

4 Cut out three fins from the sheet like this.

5 Stick them on to the other bottle like this.

6 When the fins are stuck on, tape the top of the cut bottle onto the bottom of the other bottle to make a nose cone.

7 Half-fill the bottle with water and replace the nozzle. Keep the cap on the nozzle until you are ready for take-off.

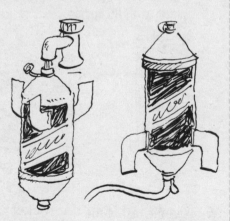

8 To launch your rocket, take the cap off the bottom nozzle, push the adapter in, turn the rocket upside down and put it on the launch pad. Attach the pump to the adapter and pump very hard! Watch your rocket shoot up!

Step 4 ....

When you've got your rocket stages built, you have to get the whole thing ready for take-off. Here's a handy checklist of what you'll need to prepare for take-off.

TAKE OFF CHECKLIST

✳ A vehicle assembly building. This is a building where the three stages of the rocket and the command module (where you'll sit) are put together. The one for the original Moon landing was the biggest building in the world – but you could use the garden shed.

> Do you really need the lawn mower at the moment?

✳ A tower to hold the rocket upright when it's all put together. This should have a lift in the side for you and your fellow astronauts to get up the 100 metres to the command module.

✳ A heat-resistant launch pad. The heat from the rockets when you take off is so strong that it could set fire to a carpet five kilometres away. (So I hope you've got a BIG garden!)

✳ The most enormous pipes you can find, to pump the millions of gallons of fuel into the tanks of each rocket stage. You'll also need lots of people to help you do this.

✳ Computers – to keep the rocket flying on the right course. Your home PC will be fine for this – it is far more powerful than the ones used on the first Moon mission.

✳ An escape pod with parachutes attached just in case something goes wrong. This will lift you out of any danger and bring you back safely to Earth.

✳ A command centre with friends who can chat to you on the radio, see where you're going, and count down from ten so that you know when you're going to take off!

You should take great care building your command module because you and two friends are going to be living there for over a week, so make it as comfy as possible. Unfortunately, it's only a little bit bigger than a small car and you've got to eat, wash, sleep and work in it – no beds or sofas, I'm afraid. If you don't want to return to Earth as a Sunday roast, make sure you cover the outside of your command module with lots of heat-resistant coverings. It's the only bit of the rocket that comes back to Earth, and when it falls into the atmosphere, it heats it up so much that it becomes white-hot! Finally, you need to attach a parachute to the module, so that you fall gently into the sea instead of splashing down so hard that you're flattened.

Put the command module right at the top of the rocket. Underneath it, you need to build a service module. This carries fuel, water and oxygen, and has a little rocket that powers you back to Earth from the Moon. So don't forget this bit!

The top bit of the command module is the lunar module. This is the only bit of the rocket that will land on the Moon. You need to make it out of aluminium because it is light. There are two parts – a descent stage, which stays on the Moon for ever afterwards, and an ascent stage which lets you get back to the command module and go home. The legs are full of honeycomb (like in a beehive) to break the impact of landing. Cover the whole thing with another sheet of aluminium to protect you from any nasty meteorites that might come thudding into you!

Finally, why not build a car called a lunar rover? It has to be really small and light, so that you can carry it in the lunar module. Wire wheels are best on the rocky, dusty lunar surface. Make sure you take some

That's hardly a lunar rover, is it?

navigational equipment or have your friend in the command module directing you from space, because everything on the Moon looks almost the same. You could easily get lost. To power your car, you need solar panels. You can find these on roofs for heating water, on on solar-powered calculators.

Other things you might like to take with you:

- ✳ a flag, so people know you've been
- ✳ a video camera
- ✳ golf clubs and balls – golf on the Moon would be really fun!

Step 5 All ready for take-off?...............

Take-off will be the most frightening thing you'll ever do, and the noise will be the loudest sound you'll ever hear – so I hope you haven't forgotten your earplugs. The speed you take off at pushes you back so hard that your face feels like jelly and wobbles around. (Luckily it doesn't stay like that afterwards.) After a few minutes the pressure eases off, and if you undo your seatbelt, you will float up out of your seat. Look out of the window – you're in space!

Step 6 ....

Congratulations – the rocket has reached the Moon! Now, one of you must decide to stay in orbit around the Moon in the command module while the other two can take the lunar module down to the Moon's surface.

When you've finally made it down to the Moon, you'll see that the scenery is a bit dull, but there are loads of fun things you can do, such as:

✳ making important speeches

✳ placing your flag in the dusty ground (you have to spread the flag out with wire as there is no wind on the Moon)

✳ jumping very high

✳ climbing high mountains with no effort at all

* driving your Moon buggy
* collecting samples – don't go home without some of the famous Moon rock!

A PRESENT FROM THE MOON

Step 7 ....

Time to head for home! Lift off in your lunar module and join up again with your colleague in orbit, before blasting off through space on your return journey to planet Earth.

So far so good. But now you face one of the most dangerous parts of your Moon mission – getting safely back through the Earth's atmosphere. As soon as your space capsule enters the Earth's atmosphere, it begins to fall so quickly towards the ground that friction from the air makes your rocket white-hot! Luckily, you've remembered to cover the outside of your rocket with a heatproof covering, haven't you?

Finally, if you carried on falling all the way to the ground, you would be flattened! This is where your parachute comes in handy. (You did remember your parachute, didn't you?) Opening the parachute of your space capsule should slow you down enough to let you splash down into the sea, where you can be rescued.

So now you know how to build a rocket to get to the Moon and what you need to survive there. No one has set foot on the Moon since the Americans left it in 1972, but soon that might change. Several countries are working on a new international space station. They're also developing reusable rockets which slow down when they come back to Earth by using rotor blades on the side. A manned mission to Mars is also being planned, which would be easier if people had a Moon base. Less fuel would be needed to blast into space from the Moon than the Earth, and there wouldn't be as far to go.

The time will come when a Moon base is built, and when it does, you'll know how to build a rocket to get there, how to train as an astronaut, and what you're letting yourself in for when you arrive.